My Earth & Space Science Library

Land Tour

Lisa J. Amstutz

Rourke Educational Media

A Division of
Carson Dellosa Education®

ROURKE'S
SCHOOL to HOME
CONNECTIONS
BEFORE AND DURING READING ACTIVITIES

Before Reading: *Building Background Knowledge and Vocabulary*

Building background knowledge can help children process new information and build upon what they already know. Before reading a book, it is important to tap into what children already know about the topic. This will help them develop their vocabulary and increase their reading comprehension.

Questions and Activities to Build Background Knowledge:

1. Look at the front cover of the book and read the title. What do you think this book will be about?
2. What do you already know about this topic?
3. Take a book walk and skim the pages. Look at the table of contents, photographs, captions, and bold words. Did these text features give you any information or predictions about what you will read in this book?

Vocabulary: *Vocabulary Is Key to Reading Comprehension*

Use the following directions to prompt a conversation about each word.
- Read the vocabulary words.
- What comes to mind when you see each word?
- What do you think each word means?

Vocabulary Words:
- *erosion*
- *plateau*
- *plates*
- *valleys*

During Reading: *Reading for Meaning and Understanding*

To achieve deep comprehension of a book, children are encouraged to use close reading strategies. During reading, it is important to have children stop and make connections. These connections result in deeper analysis and understanding of a book.

Close Reading a Text

During reading, have children stop and talk about the following:
- Any confusing parts
- Any unknown words
- Text to text, text to self, text to world connections
- The main idea in each chapter or heading

Encourage children to use context clues to determine the meaning of any unknown words. These strategies will help children learn to analyze the text more thoroughly as they read.

When you are finished reading this book, turn to the last page for an **After Reading Activity**.

Table of Contents

What Is a Landform?

Landforms are different kinds of land that make up Earth's surface.

They can be big or small.

Let's take a tour!

Types of Landforms

Some places have high mountains. They stretch to the clouds.

mountains

basin

Basins are bowl shapes in Earth's surface. Some are filled with water.

Some places have hills. Hills are smaller than mountains.

Some places are smooth and flat.
These places are called plains.

Valleys are dips between hills and mountains.

Canyons are valleys with steep sides.

A **plateau** rises above the land around it. It has a flat top.

An island is a piece of land with water all around it.

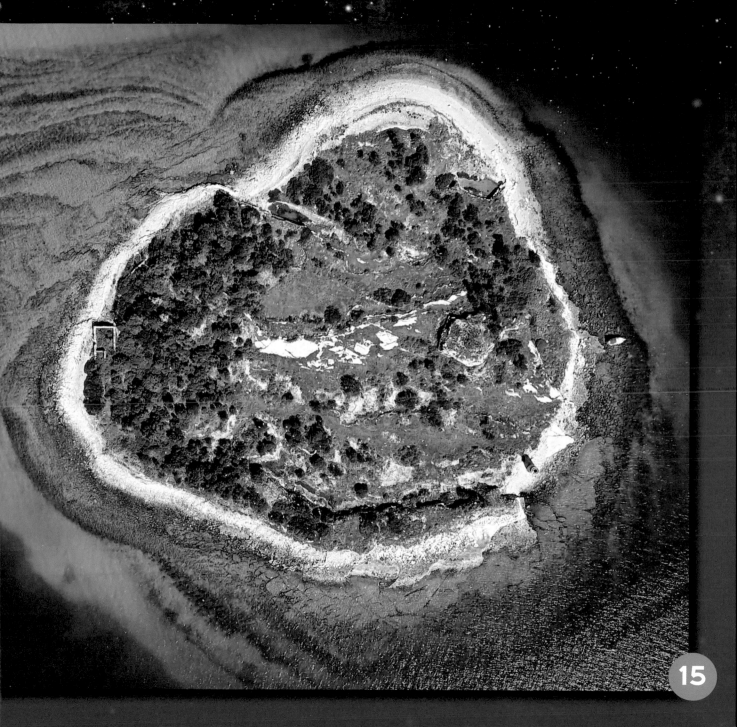

Always Moving

Landforms can change size and shape.

The **plates** that make up Earth's outer layer are always moving.

The movement makes mountains and valleys.

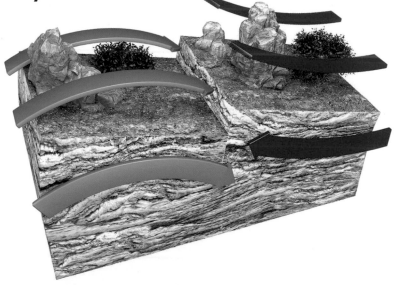

This line in the land is where two plates meet.

Wind and water also shape the land. They wear away soil and rock. This is called **erosion**.

19

Humans shape Earth too. They move rocks and soil. They create hills and basins.

This machine is a type of earthmover.

erosion (i-ROH-zhuhn): The wearing away of something by water or wind.

plateau (pla-TOH): An area of level ground that is higher than the area around it.

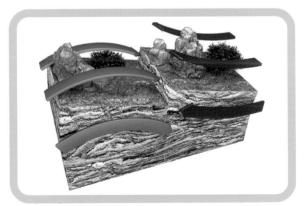

plates (playts): The flat, rigid, rocky pieces that make up Earth's outer crust.

valleys (VAL-eez): Low areas of land between hills or mountains.

Slowing Erosion

Over time, water causes erosion. Do you think soil will erode the fastest under gravel, grass, or more soil?

Supplies

2-liter bottles, emptied and cleaned (3)

sharp knife   tray   soil   gravel   cut grass   bowls (3)

Directions

1. Ask an adult to cut a rectangle from the side of each bottle. Set the bottles on their sides on a tray.

2. Put the same amount of soil in each bottle. Fill it about two-thirds full.

3. Cover the soil in one bottle with gravel. Lay the grass on the soil in the second bottle. Leave the soil in the third bottle uncovered.

4. Hold a bowl under the mouth of each bottle. Pour water over the soil. Catch the runoff in the bowl.

5. Observe: How much soil erodes from each bottle? Which bottle released the most eroded soil? The least?

Index

About the Author

Lisa J. Amstutz is the author of more than 100 children's books. She loves learning about science and sharing fun facts with kids. Lisa lives on a small farm with her family, two goats, a flock of chickens, and a dog named Daisy.

After Reading Activity

How many landforms can you find near your home? Do you see hills or plains? Do you see valleys or mountains? Make a list.

Library of Congress PCN Data

Land Tour / Lisa J. Amstutz
(My Earth and Space Science Library)
ISBN (hard cover)(alk. paper) 978-1-73163-845-8
ISBN (soft cover) 978-1-73163-922-6
ISBN (e-Book) 978-1-73163-999-8
ISBN (e-Pub) 978-1-73164-076-5
Library of Congress Control Number: 2020930190

Rourke Educational Media
Printed in the United States of America
01-1942011937

Edited by: Hailey Scragg
Cover design by: Rhea Magaro-Wallace
Interior design by: Jen Bowers
Photo Credits: Cover logo: frog © Eric Phol, test tube © Sergey Lazarev, p4 © sturti, p5 © Gregory E. Clifford, p6 © Tetiana Garkusha, p8 © helivideo, p9 © Gary Tognoni, p10 & p22 © Matt Anderson, p11 © Arpad Benedek, p12 & p 22 © Alex Potemkin, p 13 © jacquesvandinteren, p14 © tobiasjo, p15 © rusm, p16 & p22 © Naeblys, p17 © Andypott, p18 & p22 © tracielouise, p20 © CUHRIG, p21 © MarinaZg, All interior images from istockphoto.com.